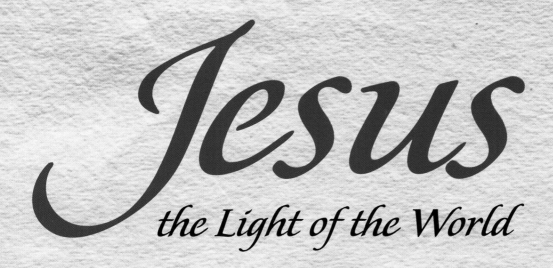

Jesus
the Light of the World

Written by

Selwyn Hughes

Paintings by Larry Dyke

BROADMAN
&HOLMAN
PUBLISHERS

NASHVILLE, TENNESSEE

© 1999
Text copyright by Selwyn Hughes
Illustrations copyright by Larry Dyke,
Somerset House Publishing, Houston, Texas
All rights reserved
Printed in Mexico

0-8054-2089-4
Published by Broadman & Holman Publishers, Nashville, Tennessee
Editorial Team: Leonard G. Goss, John Landers, Sandra Bryer
Page Design: Paul T. Gant Art & Design
Typesetting: TF Designs

Dewey Decimal Classification: 242.2
Subject Heading: DEVOTIONAL EXERCISES

Unless otherwise indicated, all Scripture references are from the
Holy Bible, New International Version (NIV)
Copyright © 1973, 1978, 1984 by the International Bible Society.

Every Day Light™

Text published in Britain as
Every Day with Jesus: The Light of the World copyright 1998

1 2 3 4 5 03 02 01 00 99

National Distributors

UK (and countries not listed below)
CWR, PO Box 230, Farnham, Surrey GU9 8XG Tel: 01252 784710 Outside UK (44) 1252 784710
AUSTRALIA: CMC Australasia, PO Box 519, Belmont,Victoria 3216 Tel: (03) 5241 3288
CANADA: CMC Distribution Ltd., PO Box 7000, Niagara on the Lake, Ontario L0S 1J0
  Tel: 1 800 325 1297
GHANA: Challenge Enterprises, PO Box 5723, Accra. Tel: (21) 222437/223249
HONG KONG: Cross Communications Ltd, Flat B, 11/F, KO's House, 577 Nathan Road, Kowloon
  Tel: 852 2780 1188/2384 0880
INDIA: Full Gospel Literature Stores, 254 Kilpauk Garden Road, Chennai 600010
  Tel: (44) 644 3073
KENYA: Keswick Bookshop, PO Box 10242, Nairobi Tel: (02) 331692/226047
MALAYSIA: Salvation Book Centre (M), 23 Jalan SS2/64, Sea Park, 47300 Petaling Jaya, Selangor Tel: (3) 7766411
NEW ZEALAND: CMC New Zealand Ltd., Private Bag, 17910 Green Lane, Auckland
  Toll free: 0800 333639
NIGERIA: FBFM, (Every Day with Jesus), Prince's Court, 37 Ahmed Onibudo Street, PO Box 70952, Victoria Island
  Tel: 01 2617721, 616832, 4700218
PHILIPPINES: Praise Incorporated, 145 Panay Avenue, Cor Sgt Esguerra St, Quezon City Tel: 632 920 5291
REPUBLIC OF IRELAND: Scripture Union, 40 Talbot Street, Dublin 1 Tel: (01) 8363764
SINGAPORE: Campus Crusade Asia Ltd., 315 Outram Road, 06–08 Tan Boon Liat Building, Singapore 169074 Tel:
  (65) 222 3640
SOUTH AFRICA: Struik Christian Books (Pty Ltd), PO Box 193, Maitland 7405, Cape Town
  Tel: (021) 551 5900
SRI LANKA: Christombu Investments, 27 Hospital Street, Colombo 1 Tel: (1) 433142/328909
TANZANIA: City Christian Bookshop, PO Box 33463, Dar es Salaam. Tel: (51) 28915
UGANDA: New Day Ltd, PO Box 2021, Kampala. Tel: (41) 255377
USA: CMC Distribution, PO Box 644, Lewiston, New York 14092-0644 Tel: 1 800 325 1297

Contents

Into the Light

About two thousand years ago Jesus Christ uttered one of His greatest sayings when He declared: "I am the light of the world." Who else in history could have framed such a sentence—and expected to be believed? Some have dismissed His words as the musings of a madman, but over the centuries multiplied millions have come to grasp the profound truth that lies behind that statement.

What did Jesus Christ have in mind, I wonder, when He made that staggering statement? What is light anyway? In one sense it is a mystery. The nearest our scientists can get to it is to tell us that light consists of three primary colors—red, green, and blue. However mysterious light may be, everyone knows that light has a revealing quality. The dictionary has a number of definitions of light, my favorite being: "Light is the agent by which objects are rendered visible." How glad we are when we find ourselves enshrouded by darkness to reach for an electric light switch or a flashlight.

No one feels comfortable in the dark, even though we learn to accustom ourselves to it. People stumble in the dark, lose direction, and some with a fear of the dark see every shadow as a spectre and every movement as ghostly.

We have invented things to make the dark less threatening—oil lamps, candles, flashlights. When light shines in the darkness, it shows that the imagined terrors have no objective reality. One writer puts it like this: "Light reveals power and beauty, and if there is something to be feared the light shows it in proportionate relation to all that is not to be feared. We do not live in darkness but in light. We are not cursed, we are blessed."[1]

When Jesus Christ made His famous statement, "I am the light of the world," He also went on to say, "So if you follow me, you won't be stumbling through the darkness, for living light will flood your path" (John 8:12 TLB). Clearly He viewed the world as a dark place and implied that those who followed Him would find in His words and teaching a flood of light to guide their path.

A famous picture painted in the middle of the nineteenth century by Holman Hunt is entitled "Jesus—the Light of the World." It portrays Jesus Christ, thorn-crowned, carrying a lantern and knocking at a closed door. How I wish I could paint a picture which would capture on canvas the thoughts that come to my mind as I ponder that staggering statement of Jesus: "I am the light of the world." Having no skill, however, with a brush, I pick up my pen to paint a word picture of how the Savior has brought light to this darkened planet.

No informed person can deny that the human race walks in darkness. Many competent observers, not given to pessimism, despair of

our race and suggest that we are not only a people who walk in darkness but a people who walk in darkness to their destruction.

It is a deep conviction of mine (as well as of millions of Christians worldwide) that Jesus Christ is light at the place of the world's darkest and most difficult problems. His life and teachings shine like a giant flashlight into the dark corners of our human predicament.

For over forty-five years now I have worked as a counselor attempting to help people who are looking for a sympathetic heart and an objective mind as they struggle with life's problems. When reminiscing recently about the issues which had been discussed with me in the counseling room, I recalled that in many of the therapy sessions I had conducted certain matters seemed to be present in people's minds.

I did not notice their persistency at first, nor was I always aware of their urgency, but experience has conditioned me to expect them and be ready to address them. What are these recurring questions? You might think they would be issues like: "How do I deal with life's difficulties?" or, "What steps should I have taken to avoid finding myself in this position?" But no. The questions were more existential ones—questions about God, the purpose of life, what lies beyond death, and so on.

I have found, over the years, five recurring problems on which people have sought some light and illumination. How glad I have been when attempting to answer their questions that I could point them to the light which comes from Jesus Christ.

The question asked most often is this: *Who is God and what is He like?* Some have put it like this: "What lies behind the universe—chance, a blind unreasoning fate, or is some sinister and horrible power in charge?" Jesus Christ has a clear answer. He is the great Illuminator (as we shall see) when it comes to telling us who God is and what He is like.

There is a wonderful story of a little boy who stood in front of a picture of his absent father, and then turned to his mother and said wistfully, "I wish Father would step out of the picture." That little boy expressed in his own way the greatest hope and desire of all who believe in the existence of God—that He would step out of the picture-frame of the universe and reveal Himself more personally, more intimately.

I heard the well-known actor and humorist Woody Allen ask in a monologue he once gave: "Why doesn't God reveal Himself more clearly? If only He would say something, give me a sign that He is there . . . if He would only cough . . . or get my Uncle Shasha to pick up the check . . ."

Tracing God's tracks

The truth is, of course, that God, the eternal Creator, has revealed Himself to us. He has shown Himself, for example, in His creation. The very first words we read when we open the Bible are these: "In the beginning God created the heavens and the earth." Is it, therefore, surprising that His creation should bear witness to Him?

I have always loved the story of the Bedouin who invited a passing traveler into his tent for some refreshment. During the course of the meal, the conversation turned to the matter of God.

"Do *you* believe in God?" questioned the traveler.

"Yes, I do," replied the Bedouin.

"But how do you know God exists when you can't see him?" asked the traveler.

The Bedouin took the traveler outside the tent and, pointing to some camel tracks in the sand, said: "How do I know it was a camel and not a horse that passed my tent last night? I know because of its tracks."

Then pointing to the sun that was beginning to set in a sea of glorious color, he added: "There are the tracks of a great and awesome God." God can be seen in His creation, but we must understand that all we know of God from creation is not all that *can* be known. Expressive though creation is in its most beautiful parts, it cannot fully reveal Him.

A Message in Writing

Another way God has revealed Himself to us is through the pages of the Bible—the Judeo-Christian Scriptures. We describe the Bible in that way because the Old Testament is a collection of documents which tells us mainly about God's dealings with the Jewish nation. The New Testament is the record of the coming of Jesus Christ to this world and His impact upon the ages. When both these books are bound together in one volume, they are referred to as "The Bible," meaning *the books*, taken from the Greek word *biblia*. Christians view the Bible as containing everything God wants us to know about how to live in an intimate relationship with Him here on earth and how to prepare for a future life with Him after we die.

The Bible reveals much more of God than creation does. Stars are lovely to look at but they can't speak. Mountains are marvellous and majestic but they can't communicate with words. Flowers are beautiful but they can't convey a written message. The first thing we look for when someone sends us flowers is the accompanying note or card. It is the words written on the note that make the gesture personal.

In the
Bible God speaks
to us in human lan-
guage about Himself
and His concern for cre-
ation—and He does so in
a variety of ways. In one of
the Gospels, for example, we
read three fascinating stories
which Jesus Himself told. One is
about a lost sheep, another about
a lost coin, and the third about
a lost son. The first story
tells of a shepherd with
a hundred sheep
who loses one
and goes in

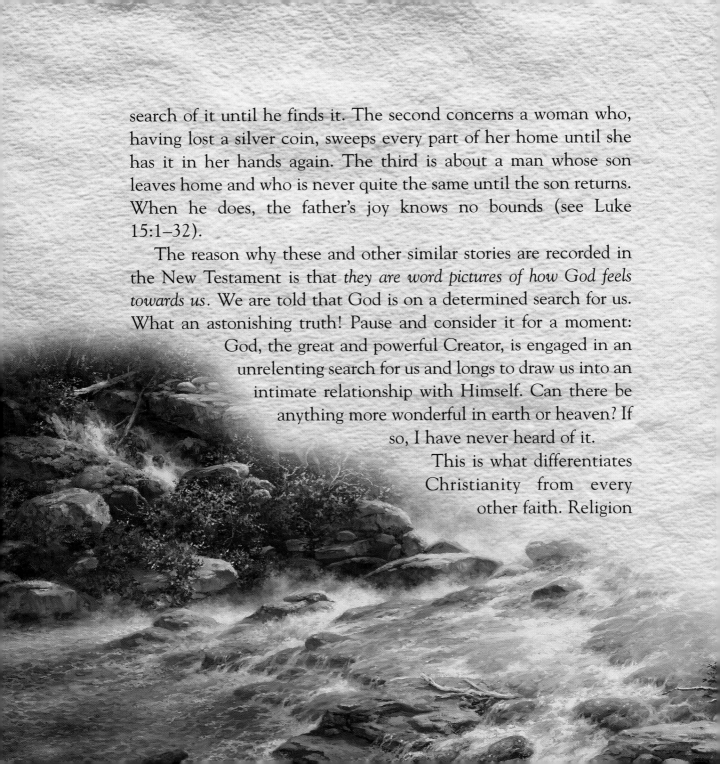

search of it until he finds it. The second concerns a woman who, having lost a silver coin, sweeps every part of her home until she has it in her hands again. The third is about a man whose son leaves home and who is never quite the same until the son returns. When he does, the father's joy knows no bounds (see Luke 15:1–32).

The reason why these and other similar stories are recorded in the New Testament is that *they are word pictures of how God feels towards us.* We are told that God is on a determined search for us. What an astonishing truth! Pause and consider it for a moment: God, the great and powerful Creator, is engaged in an unrelenting search for us and longs to draw us into an intimate relationship with Himself. Can there be anything more wonderful in earth or heaven? If so, I have never heard of it.

This is what differentiates Christianity from every other faith. Religion is mankind searching for God; Christianity is God searching for mankind. The Greek philosopher Plato is recorded as saying, "The author of the universe is hard to find." Yet in these three heart-warming stories which Jesus told, the Savior flings back the dark curtains that hide the Creator from us and lets the light in on the true nature of the Almighty.

He is a God with a shepherd's heart who searches for the lost sheep until He finds them. And in the story of the woman who sweeps the house for the lost coin, we are told that God will sweep the universe with the broom of His love until He finds that last soul. For just as a king or queen's image is stamped on a coin, so is the divine image engraved on every human soul, lost though that soul may be as a result of sin. It is true that in the story of the father whose son left home the father did not follow him, but his love was with him there, nevertheless, in the far-off country. And it was the father's love that, like a magnet, pulled him toward home.

Like Father, like Son

While both creation and the Bible are vehicles through which God reveals Himself, I want to tell you now about another way, an even greater way, in which God chose to make Himself known. *He revealed Himself to us through Jesus Christ His Son*. Think again about the story I told earlier of the little boy who longed for his absent father and said, "I wish Father would step out of the picture." You will remember that this little boy expressed in his own way the greatest hope and desire of all who believe in the existence of God—that He would step out of the picture-frame of the universe and reveal Himself more personally, more intimately.

Well, the Father has stepped out of the

picture. This is the glorious truth that Christians celebrate at Christmas—God's entrance into this world in the person of His Son, Jesus Christ.

One day when Jesus was here on earth, one of His closest followers, a man by the name of Philip, turned to Him and said, "Show us the Father, and that will be enough for us." Jesus answered him, "Anyone who has seen me has seen the Father" (John 14:8–9). In other words, "When you look at Me and at My nature and character, you are looking at the nature and character of the Father."

A striking verse in the New Testament reads thus: "No one has ever seen God, but God the One and Only, who is at the Father's side, has made him known" (John 1:18). Another verse says, "The Word became flesh and made his dwelling among us. We have seen his glory, the glory of the One and Only, who came from the Father, full of grace and truth" (John 1:14).

You will notice in the last verse I quoted that Jesus is referred to as "the Word." This term perhaps more than any other enables us to grasp just how He is able to reveal God to us. As you have taken hold of my words in the pages of this book, so you have

taken hold of my thoughts. Leaving these pages blank in the hope that you might guess my thoughts would be, I am sure you will agree, a fruitless exercise. How can you get hold of my thoughts? By getting hold of my words. When you listen to the words of Jesus Christ, you are hearing through those words the very thoughts of God. The Father and the Son are one, and when Jesus speaks He unfolds the thoughts of the Father. The Son reveals Him.

Creation, as we saw, gives us a picture of God, but it is not a perfect picture. The Old Testament tells us much more about God than creation does. With overpowering intensity Hebrew prophets such as Isaiah, Jeremiah, and Ezekiel tell us not only how passionately they believed in Him but how awesome were His ways. Some of the Old Testament writers even went so far as to believe that the great Creator of the universe might be called a Father.

One of them wrote this: "As a father has compassion on his children, so the LORD has compassion on those who fear him" (Ps. 103:13). They reached that point, but farther than that they could not go. In their hearts this longing, I fancy, could easily have taken shape: "I wish the Father would step out of the picture." They were saying in effect, "I wish the Creator could become real. Real to us." What they longed for was a personal revelation of the unseen.

Because we are personal beings, there is something within us that longs for a personal approach. Tulsi Das, one of India's poets, wrote these words: "The Impersonal laid no hold on my heart." It never does, for the human heart is personal and craves a personal response. Principles are fine, but they are no substitute for the personal. Suppose a child staying away from home wakes up in the middle of the night and cries for his parent. What do you think would happen if the person looking after him said, "Don't cry, let me tell you about the principle of parenthood"? Would the child's tears be dried and his face light up? No, because the child wants not a principle or a picture but a person—his mother or father.

The Christian faith teaches that Jesus, whom all intelligent people admire, and whose life even some non-Christians acknowledge was faultless, is none other than God in human form. The New Testament uses these phrases to describe Him: "the exact representation of [God's] being" (Heb. 1:3) and "the living God . . . in a body" (1 Tim. 3:15–16). There are many more. A little Indian boy put it beautifully when asked by his Sunday school teacher to describe Jesus. This was his reply: "Jesus is the best photograph God ever had taken." He is.

Many philosophers have struggled to define God and tell us what He is like. Well, we don't have to struggle any more—God is like Jesus. He and the Father are one, one in essence and one in unity. Jesus puts a face on God. Draw lines from Jesus into infinity and you come to a God who is just like Jesus—loving, tender, forgiving, compassionate, and just.

A mother describes how she saw her little son drawing some pictures in his copy book. "What are you drawing?" she asked. "I am drawing a picture of God," he told her. "But no one knows what God looks like," exclaimed the mother. "They will when I have finished," the child answered confidently. Yet all attempts to show what God is like, however well intended, are futile. The only one who can tell us who God is and what He is like is Jesus.

And who is God? He is our Creator, our Sustainer, our Provider. But more than that, He is the Father of our Lord Jesus Christ. Of all the statements that Jesus used to describe His Father when He was here on earth, none is greater than this. It goes right to the heart of who God is—eternal love: "For God so loved the world that he gave his one and only Son, that whoever believes in him shall not perish but have eternal life" (John 3:16).

Jesus Christ has once and for all explained who God is and what He is like. I don't know about you, but for that I am deeply grateful.

Life in Perspective

Another of the difficult issues on which men and women want light to be thrown is the problem of human existence. Often in the counseling room these questions have been put to me: What is this human life? Why are we here? What does it all mean? Here too, as I shall explain in a moment, the light that comes from Jesus Christ penetrates the darkness.

Many have struggled with the issue of "Who am I, and why am I here?" A story is told about Schopenhauer, the distinguished German philosopher, who spent most of his life brooding on the mystery of existence and could never make up his mind why he was here and what he was doing in the world. One day he was sitting on a bench in the Tiergarten in Frankfurt when the park keeper, disliking his disheveled appearance and thinking him a tramp, accosted him and asked, "Who are you?" The philosopher, interrupted in his reverie, looked up and answered: "Who am I? Who am I? I wish to God I knew."

This has been the dilemma of most of the humanistic philosophers of past centuries. They have found no real answer for the question "Who am I?" They didn't know what to make of human nature. We are no better if we turn to modern humanistic philosophers. If you ask them, "What do you make of life?" you are likely to get the answer: "Life is an eddying speck of dust, a harassed, driven leaf."

There is a saying in psychology that you don't know who you are until you know whose you are. Research has shown that children who lack a close relationship with their parents often struggle with their identity. The sense of belonging we get through connection with those who nurture us helps us to understand who we are. We are to whom we belong. And if this is true in a physical and psychological sense, it is even more true in a spiritual sense. The Bible teaches that we were created by God and for God. Only when we develop a close relationship with Him do we come to know ourselves—who we are and why we are here. Where there is no knowledge of God, then the soul feels orphaned and life is drained of all meaning.

For centuries men and women have been trying to

manage human life without God. They have tried to thrust Him out of the universe which He has made. People tend to laugh at preachers and tell them to drop their silly patter about salvation and the need to know God. They say such things as, "Man has no Savior but himself . . . if we must have religion then it must be a religion without revelation . . . a religion of humanity and not a religion of God."

The poet William Ernest Henley put it like this:

> Out of the night that covers me,
> Black as the pit from pole to pole,
> I thank whatever gods there be
> For my unconquerable soul. . . .
> It matters not how straight the gate,
> How charged with punishment the scroll,
> I am the master of my fate, I am the captain of my soul.

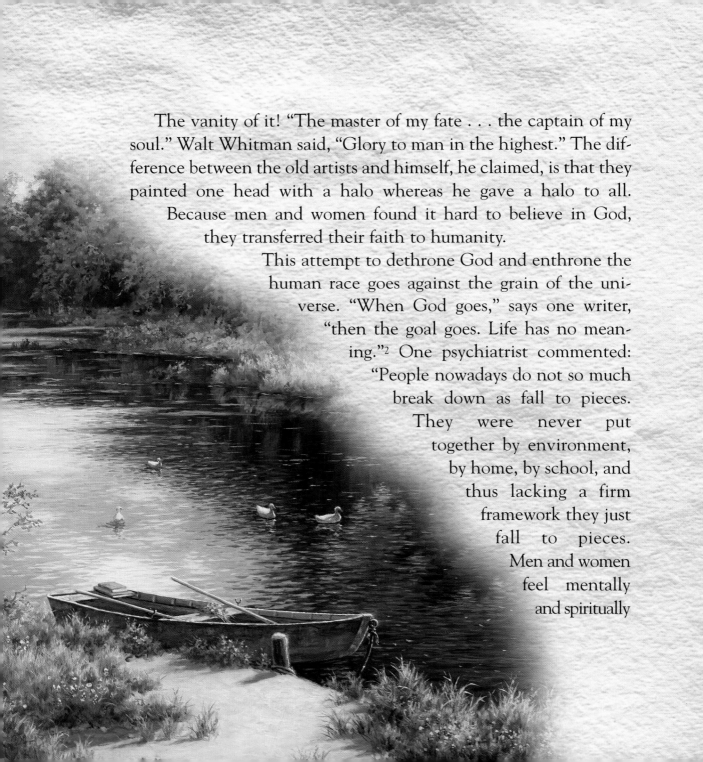

The vanity of it! "The master of my fate . . . the captain of my soul." Walt Whitman said, "Glory to man in the highest." The difference between the old artists and himself, he claimed, is that they painted one head with a halo whereas he gave a halo to all. Because men and women found it hard to believe in God, they transferred their faith to humanity.

This attempt to dethrone God and enthrone the human race goes against the grain of the universe. "When God goes," says one writer, "then the goal goes. Life has no meaning."[2] One psychiatrist commented: "People nowadays do not so much break down as fall to pieces. They were never put together by environment, by home, by school, and thus lacking a firm framework they just fall to pieces. Men and women feel mentally and spiritually sick because they are lost. The old landmarks have been obliterated and they don't know how to find their way about in a universe of this kind." He added: "Like a blind man tapping with his stick on the sidewalk so mankind is tapping from event to event trying to find the way home."

Yet despite the darkness a bright light shines. It is the light of Jesus Christ. Listen to His prescription for finding meaning: "Seek first his [God's] kingdom and his righteousness, and all these things will be given to you as well" (Matt. 6:33). In other words, put God first and then all other things will fall into place.

Our Homing Instinct

It has been said that "there is only one sickness and that is homesickness." People today may not realize it, but this is their chief ailment—they are homesick. They were made by God and for God, and without a knowledge of Him there is restlessness in the human heart that can never be resolved.

Students of natural history know about the wonderful instinct of direction displayed by animals which is sometimes called the homing instinct. Cats and dogs often find their way across huge stretches of unknown country. Swallows and other migrant birds fly confidently to countries thousands of miles away. Salmon return to spawn in the rivers of their birth. Nothing in all nature is more wonderful than this amazing instinct of the lower creation to return home.

It is my belief that deep in the heart of every one of us there is a homing instinct—profound, personal, and impossible to eradicate. Though we may ignore and even deny it, our hearts will never find true satisfaction until we enter into a relationship with the One who created us. Augustine, one of the great Christian leaders of the fourth and fifth centuries, summed it up in this poignant phrase: "Thou hast made us for Thyself and our hearts are restless till they find their rest in Thee."

The truth is that there can be no sense of meaning or purpose in our lives until we find God. I base this assumption on what I think are two undeniable facts. The first is this: *there is a thirst in everyone's soul which nothing on earth can satisfy.* We may have everything the material world can offer and still feel empty, still feel that something is missing. An awareness of this resonates through every area of life.

Some time ago I read the story of Boris Becker, the noted tennis player, who came close to taking his own life because he was overwhelmed by a sense of hopelessness and lack of meaning.

31

"I had won Wimbledon twice before, once as the youngest player. I was rich. I had all the material possessions I needed; cars, women, everything . . . I know that this is a cliché: it's the old song of the movie and pop stars who commit suicide. They have everything and yet they are so unhappy. . . . I had no inner peace. I was a puppet on a string."[3]

Jack Higgins, the highly successful thriller-writer who wrote *The Eagle Has Landed,* was asked by a reporter, "Out of all the things you know now what would you have liked to have known when you were a boy?" This was his reply: "That when you get to the top there's nothing there."

Now earth may satisfy the beasts. As far as we know it does. But it does not satisfy us. One poet expressed it like this:

> In this house with starry dome,
> Floored with gemlike plains and seas,
> Shall I never feel at home,
> Never wholly at ease?[4]

Never. You weren't meant to be.

Now here is the second fact: *in every soul there is a desire to know and relate to God.* Listen to these powerful words from the poem "Intimations of Immortality" by Wordsworth in which he speaks with plainness of this reminiscence of the soul:

> Our birth is but a sleep and a forgetting.
> The Soul that rises with us, our life's Star,
> Hath had elsewhere its setting,
> And cometh from afar;
> Not in entire forgetfulness,

And not in utter nakedness,
But trailing clouds of glory do we come
From God who is our home.

"From God who is our home." There are immortal longings in every one of us, and the ache that earth cannot satisfy can be satisfied by God. All feel it, but not all understand it.

A legend from the Western Isles of Scotland tells of a sea king who longed for the company of a human being. One day while resting in his cave beneath the sea he heard a human cry, and rising to the surface he spotted a little child in a boat which was adrift. Just as he was about to make for the vessel and take the child, a rescue party intervened and he missed his prize. But, so the story goes, just as the rescuers drew away with the one so nearly lost, the sea king cupped his hand and threw into the heart of the child a little sea-salt wave. As he submerged he said to himself: "The child is mine. When he grows the sea will call him and he will come home to me at last."

This legend is not based on fact, of course, but it suggests a timeless truth—that God has put in every heart a longing for Himself. Every man and woman knows it is there, but many do not want to admit to it. This phenomenon has been noticed by philosophers and sages from the beginning of time. Plato compared human beings to leaky jars. Somehow we are always unfulfilled. We may pour things into the containers of our lives but for some reason our souls never seem to stay filled; they leak.

Listen to another statement which fell from the lips of Jesus: "If anyone is thirsty, let him come to me and drink. Whoever believes in me, as the Scripture has said, streams of living water will flow from within him" (John 7:37–38).

You want to know who you are? You are dear enough for God to send His Son into the world to give His life for you on a cross. You want to know why you are here? You are here to connect with God, to find satisfaction for your soul in Him, and to be with Him in heaven for all eternity.

The Empty Tomb

Another area of darkness which only the light that comes from Jesus Christ can illuminate is that of death. Death, it has been said, is the great enigma of life. "Humanly speaking," says one writer, "it is an insoluble mystery, the one secret of the universe which is kept, the silence which is never broken."[5]

Death is one of the rare things which can be predicted of everyone. The weary and despairing meet death as a friend, the cynical and disillusioned meet it with indifference, the happy and healthy see it as a foe. But whether it is viewed as friend, foe, or cold companion, it comes to us all. As George Bernard Shaw put it in his cryptic comment, "The statistics concerning death are very impressive." It reduces the exalted and the lowly to the common denominator of dust.

The mystery of death is as old as humanity. The earliest writings find men and women pondering the problem of the great beyond. Throughout the long history of the human race, we find people nursing their hopes on a variety of dreams, and passing in turn from belief in a fuller life, greater and grander than this, to nirvana—non-existence.

Once, when preparing to give a talk on death, I researched what some of the writers who lived in the centuries before Jesus Christ had to say concerning this great mystery. One referred to it as "the undiscovered country from which no traveler returns." Another, when asked what follows death, replied: "Nothing follows death; life goes out like a guttering candle." Others described it variously as "a dark cavern," "a blind alley," "a tunnel with no light at the other end."

When Jesus Christ came into the world, however, He shone a light into the dark cavern of death and showed it to be a mystery no more. When speaking to His disciples about His own death, He said: "Do not let your hearts be troubled. Trust in God; trust also in me. In my Father's house are many rooms; if it were not so, I would have told you. I am going there to prepare a place for you" (John 14:1–2).

There was always an engaging frankness about Jesus. Notice the phrase, "If it were not so, I would have told you." It was as if He were saying, "Do you think I would allow you to labor under a delusion? Do you think I would allow you to put faith in a falsehood? Do you think I would allow you to be misled, or entertain a baseless though comforting illusion?"

From all that we know of Jesus Christ from the Gospels, we cannot conceive of Him acting in this way toward us. We are certain that under all circumstances He would tell us the truth. Jesus, besides being the world's greatest idealist, was also an uncompromising realist. He faced up to things squarely. He got to grips with realities.

Let me cite an instance from the New Testament. A well-educated man, in a position of authority, approached Jesus and said, "Teacher, I will follow you wherever you go." What did Jesus answer? Was He swept away by this generous attachment to Himself? Not at all. He knew that the man did not understand what He was really saying. So His reply was chilling in its challenging realism: "Foxes have holes and birds of the air have nests, but the Son of Man has no place to lay his head" (Matt. 8:19–20). In other words: "If you are going to follow Me, then you need to know you will have no guaranteed bed for the night . . . there will be times when you will have to be content with sleeping in a field, or on a rock." Realism!

Or consider again how despite the Savior's explicit and oft-repeated declarations of the true character of His kingdom, the minds of the disciples continued up to the last to be dominated by dreams of imperial power. Did Jesus allow them to cherish false expectations? No. He forewarned them with the utmost frankness of what was actually to happen. This is how one Gospel writer describes it: "From that time on Jesus began to explain to his disciples that he must go to Jerusalem and suffer many things at the hands of the elders, chief priests and teachers of the law, and that he must be killed and on the third day be raised to life" (Matt. 16:21).

And so we could go on multiplying examples of the realism and candor of Jesus. But enough has been said, I hope, to show that He would never hide the truth to spare His disciples' feelings. He was frank as well as fond, candid no less than kind. When, therefore, such a person says with reference to the glories of the world to come, "If it were not so, I would have told you," we know that He means what He says and we can take Him at His word. He tells us in effect, "If seventy years of life, more or less, is all you could expect, I would be frank with you and urge you to make the most of it, but in my Father's house . . ."

Many years ago a famous scientist by the name of Professor T. H. Huxley, the man who invented the term *agnostic* and applied it to himself, passed through a brief period of intense mental and spiritual illumination that led to the swift reversal of the judgments of a lifetime. As he lay on his deathbed, his nurse reported, he experienced a dazzling revelation of the world that lies beyond. Raising himself on his elbows, his eyes sparkling and his face aglow, he gazed transported for a few moments at the scene, then sinking back on his pillow he murmured: "So it was true . . . it was true." Not all of us are privileged to be given such a vision. The splendor and glory of the world that lies beyond are not for every eye. But the reality of it is certain. If it were not so, Jesus would have told us.

41

As I have combed the record of Jesus' days on earth, I have noticed that on two separate occasions when He referred to death He used the word *sleep*. And He used it in such a way as to exclude the idea that it was a figure of speech. To the mourners standing around the breathless body of a little girl He said, "The child is not dead but asleep" (Mark 5:39). Then He proceeded to bring her back to life.

To His disciples concerning a man already laid in the grave He said: "Our friend Lazarus has fallen asleep" (John 11:11). Indeed, He told a group of people who had gathered to hear His teaching: "I tell you the truth, if anyone keeps my word, he will never see death" (John 8:51). *Sleep*, and not *death*, was the word Jesus often used to denote the end of life here on earth, and axiomatic in His teaching was the idea that life goes on.

A fate worse than death

So what did Jesus mean when He used the word *death?* Clearly He did not mean the end of our physical life. He called that "sleep." And yet sometimes He used the word *death* as we see from the words quoted above. How

did He use that darker word? He kept it in reserve for something more awful than the end of physical activity. He spoke of the death of the soul, a process of spiritual decay at work in men and women, the consequences of which are so awful that He couldn't do enough to save them. That was what broke His heart and led Him to die for us on the cross.

Jesus Christ loves men and women and has done His utmost to save them. Those who do not put their trust in Him will be banished from His presence and separated from Him for all eternity. Perhaps the most solemn words that He ever spoke are those He used to depict the future judgment when everyone will be judged according to their relationship

with Him. Those who had no real relationship with Him when they were here on earth will hear the words, "'Depart from me. . . .' Then they will go away to eternal punishment, but the righteous to eternal life" (Matt. 25:41, 46). Tough words but true.

Seeing is believing

I realize, of course, that the force of these words will depend on what view one holds of Jesus. I believe that He was God on earth, but even those who would not share that conviction have said this: "He is the best that humanity has ever seen . . . the kindest, bravest, purest soul, the founder of a faith accepted by a third of the world, a man who always spoke the truth." That being so, ought we not to scrutinize closely what He said—even when His words challenge us to the depth of our souls?

Now when it comes to Jesus' illumination of the dark cavern of death, we not only have His words; we have also the fact of His resurrection. Remember how one cynic described death: "the undiscovered country from which no traveler returns"? Well, one traveler has returned. This is how it happened.

The Gospels record that following Jesus' crucifixion in Jerusalem on that first Good Friday, His dead body was taken down from the cross and placed in a tomb. The Roman authorities placed against the entrance to the tomb a huge stone and sealed it with the seal of Rome. They did not want any of Jesus' followers to go in, steal His body, and pretend that He had not died. But something quite staggering took place.

After Jesus had been in the tomb three days, God miraculously raised Him from the dead. A group of women who came to the tomb in order to anoint His body with sweet spices (a Jewish ritual) were concerned as to how they would roll away the stone that was sealing the sepulchre, but when they got there they found it had already been rolled away. This is how one of the Gospel writers described the event:

> But when they looked up, they saw that the stone,
> which was very large, had been rolled away.
> As they entered the tomb, they saw a
> young man dressed in a

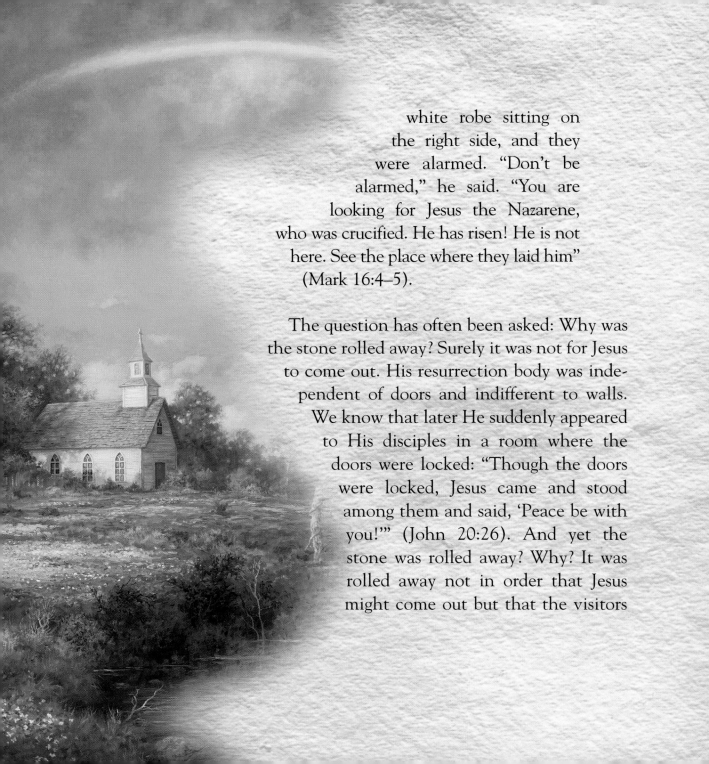

white robe sitting on the right side, and they were alarmed. "Don't be alarmed," he said. "You are looking for Jesus the Nazarene, who was crucified. He has risen! He is not here. See the place where they laid him" (Mark 16:4–5).

The question has often been asked: Why was the stone rolled away? Surely it was not for Jesus to come out. His resurrection body was independent of doors and indifferent to walls. We know that later He suddenly appeared to His disciples in a room where the doors were locked: "Though the doors were locked, Jesus came and stood among them and said, 'Peace be with you!'" (John 20:26). And yet the stone was rolled away? Why? It was rolled away not in order that Jesus might come out but that the visitors to the tomb might go in. It was not intended to be the means of His exit but of their entrance.

This is why the resurrection is more than a piece of history; it makes it also a pledge. God rolled away the stone not that His Son might come out but that everyone might know that He had risen; that the first disciples might steal into the tomb and see only "the place where they laid him."

Is the point clear? Perhaps another illustration might help. An unmarried writer with no experience of children tells how once he was asked by some friends to look after their little son for one night while they visited a sick relative. He agreed, and when it came to bedtime the man took the boy to his room and tucked him in for the night.

As he was about to leave the room the little fellow falteringly confessed that he was afraid.

"Afraid of what?" asked the man. The little boy pointed to a

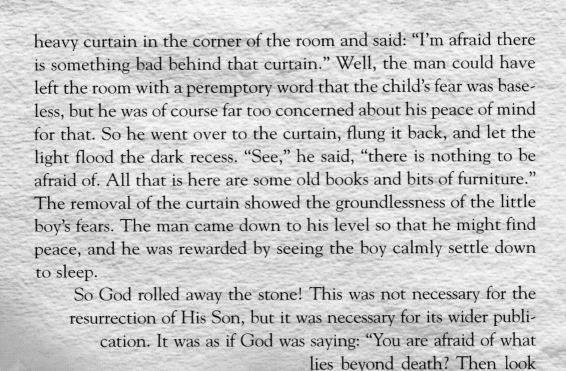

heavy curtain in the corner of the room and said: "I'm afraid there is something bad behind that curtain." Well, the man could have left the room with a peremptory word that the child's fear was baseless, but he was of course far too concerned about his peace of mind for that. So he went over to the curtain, flung it back, and let the light flood the dark recess. "See," he said, "there is nothing to be afraid of. All that is here are some old books and bits of furniture." The removal of the curtain showed the groundlessness of the little boy's fears. The man came down to his level so that he might find peace, and he was rewarded by seeing the boy calmly settle down to sleep.

So God rolled away the stone! This was not necessary for the resurrection of His Son, but it was necessary for its wider publication. It was as if God was saying: "You are afraid of what lies beyond death? Then look into the open tomb." Jesus has conquered death and, as one New

Testament writer puts it, "has brought life and immortality to light through the gospel" (2 Tim. 1:10).

For those who follow Jesus Christ, death is no longer a blind alley but a thoroughfare; no more an abysmal cavern but a tunnel. Light floods the darkness. No one who knows Jesus need be afraid of death. To be afraid of that larger life is a form of atheism. Doubt about the future means doubt about the present. It means that the Master who went down through death and came back and said, "I am the resurrection and the life. He who believes in me will live, even though he dies" (John 11:25) is not dependable. As a little bird on the twig of a tree might say to a strong wind, "All right, twist me off if you can. I have an alternative. I have wings," so a Christian can say to death, "Twist me off my earthly perch. I have an alternative. I have immortality. I have God." Nothing can shake that. Nothing!

Death may be a dark cavern, but the Great Illuminator has lit it up. We do not know a great deal about what life is like on the other side (we know some), but when we know Jesus Christ then that is enough. Then we can say with Richard Baxter:

> My knowledge of that life is small,
> The eye of faith is dim,
> But 'tis enough that Christ knows all
> And I shall be with Him.

Light in the Dark Places

We turn to think about another of life's mysterious problems: pain and suffering. I heard one doctor say that a person who is undisturbed by the problem of pain and suffering is afflicted with one of two conditions: either a hardening of the heart or a softening of the brain. He was right. Everyone who is mentally alive—especially if he believes in a God of love—finds this problem a difficult one to solve.

The explanations which some people offer of this dark mystery are shallow indeed. A preacher I know heard one person tell a woman whose son had died in a tragic car accident that God had taken him away in order to make her more patient. If that was so (and I do not believe it was), then the cure seems dreadfully out of proportion to the disease. I thought at the time I heard this story (and still do) that it was a pitiful attempt at an explanation. Better to hold one's peace than to press a motive on God which one would condemn in a human being.

Some suggest that God would cure all suffering if people would only "believe." They forget that some of the world's most notable saints have had to walk the way of suffering. Others suggest that pain and suffering are mere figments of a diseased imagination, having no basis in reality, and are curable by a readjustment of thought.

Now without doubt it is good to fill the mind with strong positive thoughts—far better than self-pity and hypochondria—but when the idea is propounded that pain or suffering is a figment of the imagination, then something within us rebels against such an imposition. The problem of suffering cannot be approached with superior forms of self-deception. It must be faced in all its hideous nakedness.

The more I have listened to the various explanations of philosophers and others as to why there is suffering, the more convinced I am that only Jesus Christ can cast light on the subject of pain and suffering. But first, consider with me some of the attempted explanations given throughout the ages by reputable men and women.

Pain and suffering are necessary in such a universe as this, claims one school of thought. In a way that is sometimes difficult to understand, joy and pain intertwine. They are not really disparate, it is said; they belong together. It is a false antithesis which sets one against the other. "In joy we are conceived," says one exponent of this theory, "but only in pain and labor were we brought forth. That God-like thing called mother-love was woven in woe." This poem by an anonymous author makes a similar point:

The cry of man's anguish went up to God,
Lord take away my pain!
The shadow that darkens this world Thou hast made;

The close coiling chain
That strangles the heart!
The burden that weighs on the wings
That would soar.
Lord take away pain from the world Thou hast made,
That it love Thee the more!

Then the Lord answered to the cry of the world;
Shall I take away pain;
And with it the power of the soul to endure;
Made strong by the strain?
Shall I take away pity that knits heart to heart.
And sacrifice high?
Will you lose all the heroes that lift from the fire
White brows to the sky?
Shall I take away the love that redeems with a price?
And smiles at its loss?
Can you spare from your lives that which would
climb into mine,
The Christ on His cross?

Another view is that from suffering comes a rich supply of sympathy that has enriched the human race. There is something insensitive in a man or woman who has not suffered, it is said. And sympathy is far too precious in this needy world to begrudge the price at which it is purchased.

Still others have maintained that as we come to understand the way in which God created us—with free will—then we begin to catch a glimpse of why we are exposed to suffering and

pain. The first human pair—Adam and Eve—disobeyed God and plunged the whole human race into chaos. We live now in a fallen world and much of what we suffer (not all) is due to our own ignorance, carelessness, or folly. An all-powerful God could have avoided this situation by making us marionettes. Can anyone regret (apart from those utterly engulfed in sorrow) that God did not take that path?

Then some try to throw light on this perplexing problem of suffering by pointing out that its power to help or hinder depends upon the reaction of the sufferer. Observant people in all ages have noticed that the same trouble in two different lives can produce diametrically opposite results. One is strangely sweetened by suffering, refined and enriched by it. Another is embittered, jaundiced, and made sour.

A Savior who suffered

But what light, we must ask ourselves, does Jesus Christ shed on this problem? The surprising thing is that never once does He attempt to give an explanation for human suffering. The light He shines on this issue comes not so much from His words but from the manner in which He faced suffering and turned it to good.

Come with me for a moment to the Garden of Gethsemane, the place where Jesus prayed as He prepared Himself for death by crucifixion. This is how the scene is recorded by Luke, one of the Gospel writers:

He withdrew about a stone's throw beyond them [His disciples], knelt down and prayed, "Father, if you are willing, take this cup from me; yet not my will, but yours be done." An angel from heaven appeared to him and strengthened him (Luke 22:41–43). Notice the words: *an angel from heaven appeared to him and strengthened him.*

Here the answer of God to His prayer was not to take away the cup—to deliver Him from the forthcoming ordeal—but to strengthen Him in such a way that He would be able to make the bitter cup of His suffering into the cup of salvation that He would put to the thirsty lips of humanity. God's answer was not exemption from suffering, but strength to use it.

The Christian faith does not promise anyone exemption from suffering. How could it when at the heart of the faith is a cross

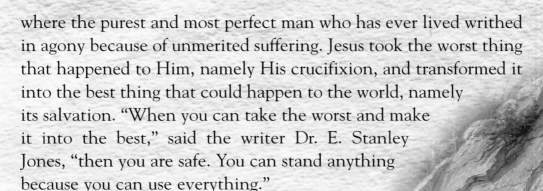

where the purest and most perfect man who has ever lived writhed in agony because of unmerited suffering. Jesus took the worst thing that happened to Him, namely His crucifixion, and transformed it into the best thing that could happen to the world, namely its salvation. "When you can take the worst and make it into the best," said the writer Dr. E. Stanley Jones, "then you are safe. You can stand anything because you can use everything."

I would be failing in my responsibility as Bible teacher if I did not point out that there are times when God miraculously intervenes in human suffering and heals individuals. A large part of Jesus' ministry when He was here on earth was devoted to healing those who were ill. That God heals through prayer is attested by thousands of people all over the world. Those who are healed rejoice, and those who are not healed are given strength to bear it. So either way they win.

It has been said that the world needs nothing so much as it needs two things: light on the *mystery* of life, and light on the *mastery* of life. Jesus gives us both, for He embodied both. Throughout the three and one-half years in which He traveled with His disciples, He demonstrated over and over again how to use everything and turn it to good. Here's an example of what I mean. The Gospel writer Luke records an occasion when, because Jesus healed someone, a group of religious leaders became incensed with Him and tried to find a way to harm Him.

> He looked around at them all, and then said to the man, "Stretch out your hand." He did so, and his hand was completely restored. But they were furious and began to discuss with one another what they might do to Jesus. One of those days Jesus went out to a mountainside to pray, and spent the night praying to God. When morning came, he called his disciples to him and chose twelve of them, whom he also designated apostles (Luke 6:10–13).

The fury of the religious leaders furthered His purposes by precipitating the decision to choose the twelve disciples with whom He could entrust His message.

Take another example. A Pharisee asked Jesus to dine with him and then omitted all the courtesies he would customarily give to a guest. He gave Him no kiss of greeting, no water for His feet, and no oil for His hair. His treatment of Jesus could be described as a social snub. It would have sent some people back to their homes with a permanent wound and a permanent hatred. But this did not happen to Jesus. He assumed moral mastery of the situation (see Luke 7:36–50).

The discourtesy of the Pharisee left a poor, despised, sinful woman to make up what the host had left undone. She came to Jesus and washed His feet with her tears and used her hair in place of a towel. Jesus then pointed out to the Pharisee how discourteous he had been, and proceeded to forgive both him and the woman. Instead of taking the role of as snubbed guest, He became the dispenser of forgiveness. He did not carry the snub; He used it. The world sits at the feet of such moral mastery and learns to live. Light for the mastery of life.

Earlier I said that Jesus Christ never once attempted to give an explanation for human suffering. Now why that should be I do not know. We do know, however, that God created the world as a perfect place in which to live and that there was no suffering before Adam and Eve sinned. Nowhere, though, in the record of Jesus' life do we find Him giving a clear solution to the problem. Instead we discover Him, as we have seen, not so much explaining the cause of suffering but meeting it head on. The light He shines on this issue of suffering, we said, is provided not so much by His words but by the manner in which He faced suffering and turned it to good.

But there is another side of this we must look at which, though it does not give us an explanation, brings great comfort to the human heart. Let me set the scene for you. A little while after Jesus had been crucified and resurrected from the dead, His disciples were gathered in a locked room. Suddenly Jesus appeared among them. How did He get in? The only explanation is that in His resurrection body He was able to pass through doors and walls without hindrance.

Thomas, one of the disciples, had some doubts about the fact that Jesus Christ had risen from the dead, and Jesus, knowing this, approached him. Pointing to the scars of crucifixion still on His body, He said to Thomas: "Put your finger here; see my hands. Reach out your hand and put it into my side. Stop doubting and believe" (John 20:27). Following that encounter with the resurrected Jesus, Thomas overcame his doubts and offered this confession: "My Lord and my God!"

What does that incident tell us? It tells us that Jesus has suffered too. Over the years I have talked to many people who have suffered, and many have

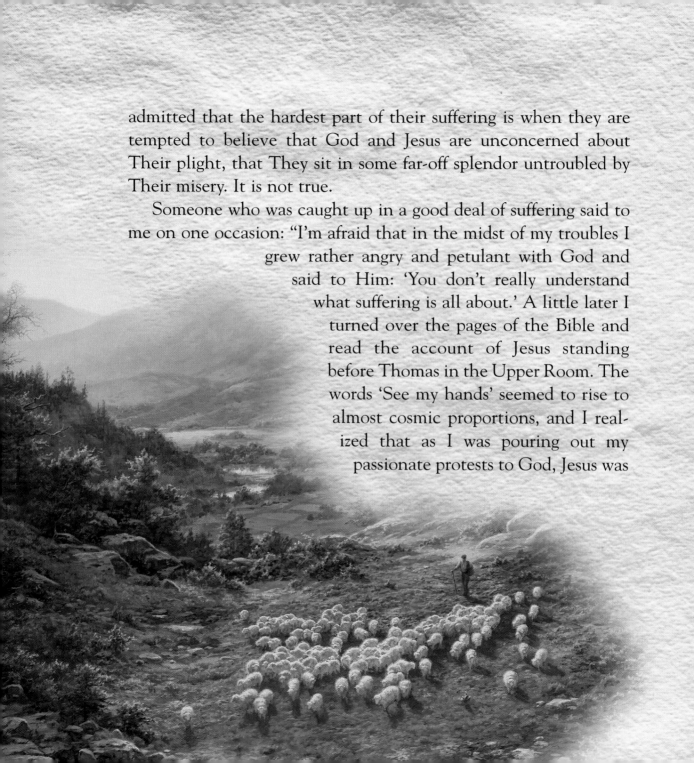

admitted that the hardest part of their suffering is when they are tempted to believe that God and Jesus are unconcerned about Their plight, that They sit in some far-off splendor untroubled by Their misery. It is not true.

Someone who was caught up in a good deal of suffering said to me on one occasion: "I'm afraid that in the midst of my troubles I grew rather angry and petulant with God and said to Him: 'You don't really understand what suffering is all about.' A little later I turned over the pages of the Bible and read the account of Jesus standing before Thomas in the Upper Room. The words 'See my hands' seemed to rise to almost cosmic proportions, and I realized that as I was pouring out my passionate protests to God, Jesus was standing there before me, unseen perhaps, but saying in effect, 'See my hands.'"

Who has suffered like Jesus? Crucifixion was the most fiendish of tortures, which took a living, breathing man and pinned him to a cross. Jesus may not give an explanation for the mystery of suffering, but He comes to all who suffer and says, "Look: I have suffered too."

Most talk about suffering by those who haven't suffered is shallow. Jesus is able to succor sufferers because He has suffered Himself. There is a kinship among all who suffer, which others cannot share. They understand each other. Some years ago, a few months after my wife had died with cancer, a friend said, "Welcome to the Fellowship of the Wounded."

We don't know exactly why God allows suffering in His world, but we do know that it can be turned to good. If God Himself came into this world and suffered in the person of His Son, then there must be some purpose in it. Perhaps we are big enough to ask the questions but not big enough to understand the answers, even if they were given us. Though we may not have all the answers we would like on the subject of pain and suffering, enough light is thrown by Jesus on the shadowed way. He Himself suffered, turned it all to good, and is able to sustain all sufferers and empower them to bear it. Never forget—the founder of the Christian faith has scarred hands!

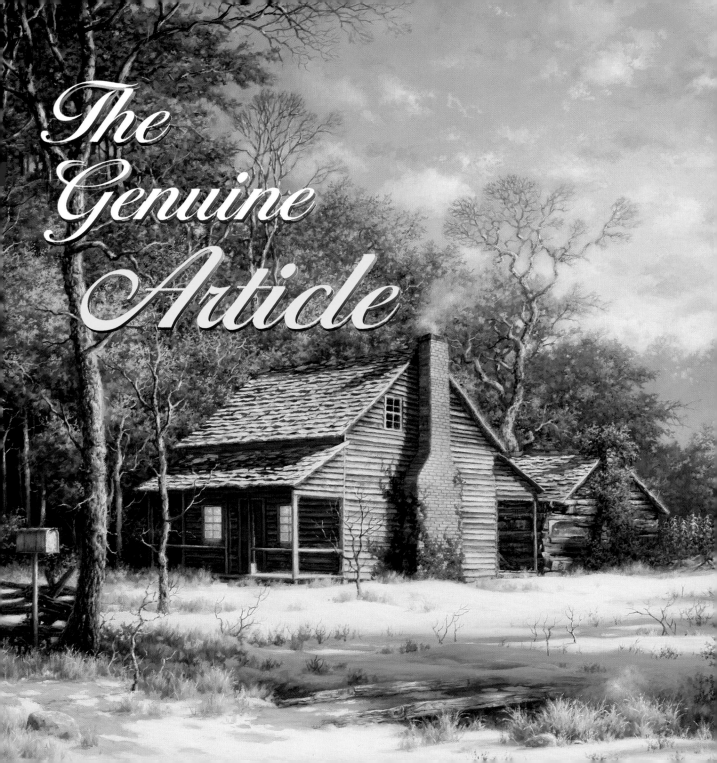

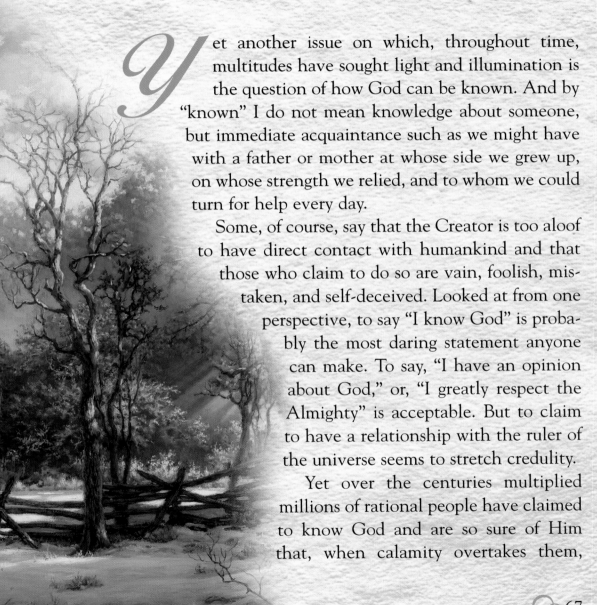

et another issue on which, throughout time, multitudes have sought light and illumination is the question of how God can be known. And by "known" I do not mean knowledge about someone, but immediate acquaintance such as we might have with a father or mother at whose side we grew up, on whose strength we relied, and to whom we could turn for help every day.

Some, of course, say that the Creator is too aloof to have direct contact with humankind and that those who claim to do so are vain, foolish, mistaken, and self-deceived. Looked at from one perspective, to say "I know God" is probably the most daring statement anyone can make. To say, "I have an opinion about God," or, "I greatly respect the Almighty" is acceptable. But to claim to have a relationship with the ruler of the universe seems to stretch credulity.

Yet over the centuries multiplied millions of rational people have claimed to know God and are so sure of Him that, when calamity overtakes them,

they are still unshaken and confidently assert their faith in Him. Face this fact: it is possible for mortals in this shadowed world to know God and to know Him intimately. Those who shut themselves off from this experience are like some poor fellow stumbling through life with his eyes closed to the light. Make no mistake about it—God can be *known*.

But how? It is generally believed that there are many paths to God. Some claim that if you live a good life, do not indulge in criminal behavior, pay strict adherence to the moral code, then you will eventually get close to God. Others claim that if you subscribe to religion, any religion, and offer worship to the Creator, that too will bring you in touch with God.

What does Jesus—the One who said, "I am the light of the world"—have to say about this issue? Once, after Jesus had been talking to His close followers about His impending return to heaven, one of them asked Him: "How can we know the way?" This was Jesus' reply: "I am the way and the truth and the life. No one comes to the Father except through me" (John 14:6). We need not walk in darkness any longer, wondering how we can get to know God. *Jesus is the way.*

What did Jesus mean when He said that He is the way to God? Perhaps this story might help. Years ago a traveler to Africa got lost in the jungle and asked a local man if he could show him the way to the next village. The local man agreed. As together they trudged through the jungle the traveler became uneasy because he could see no proper path. "Are you sure

this is the way?" he asked. His guide replied: "I am the way." The knowledge and experience of the local man got the traveler through the jungle—the guide was the *way*.

It is important to understand that Jesus is not a way to God as if there were many others. Jesus is the way. The Christian faith claims that Jesus Christ is the only way to God, and that apart from Him there is simply no other way. This idea is not something thought up by Christians; it comes from Jesus' own words about Himself. Here are His exact words: "I tell you the truth, the man who does not enter the sheep pen by the gate, but climbs in by some other way, is a thief and a robber" (John 10:1).

One of the remarks I often hear when talking to people about spiritual things is this: "But isn't one faith as good as another? Isn't there more than one way to God?" This reasoning sounds broadminded, but actually, when it is carefully examined, it is not. It must not be denied, of course, that there are fine things in other faiths—ethical teaching, for example. Christianity recognizes these commendable points and is grateful for them. What Christians claim is not that there are no good things in other world faiths, but that those good things are insufficient by themselves to save us. Jesus Christ is the only one who saves. Committed Christians are not unmindful of the light that has come from other lamps, and they do not regard themselves as personally superior to those who worship and try to find God in other ways. But because Jesus said He is the light of the world and the only way to God, then they submit to His claims and trust His truth.

The Christian faith is not one among others. It is in a category by itself. And this is why. No other world faith even claims that its great teacher was God come down to earth in human form. That is what, as we have seen, Jesus Christ claimed for Himself. He was God and came to us from God—He came all the way down to our level. There is no human need beyond His power to meet. Every spiritually sensitive person is aware of falling beneath God's standards and carrying within his or her soul, because of that, a haunting sense of guilt.

All people are aware, too, that they can do nothing about resolving that guilt. Jesus Christ died on the cross to save us from that guilt, to wash away its stain from our soul, and to open up the way to God. Every normal man and woman is in awe of death and can't escape it. Jesus conquered death and opened the way to eternal life. His invitation now is for all humanity to come to Him so they might be saved. He abides no barriers of class, race, or color.

It seems strange to people of other faiths that Christians will not allow Jesus to be included in a pantheon—an emporium of different gods. How can we? Based on what He Himself said, and believing what we do about Him, we cannot concede even by implication that there are any "gods" or prophets equal to Him. He is unique in His person and in what He accomplished when He was here on earth.

Unthinking people often say that Christianity is a Western faith forced on the East. It is not. Christianity in its origin is an Eastern faith, but in its nature it is a world faith. It is no more Europe's and America's than it is China's, India's, and Africa's. Jesus Christ is God's provision for all men and women— everywhere.

There it is. Plain questions and plain answers. Light in darkness.

Connecting with God

But we have one more issue to settle. If the only path to knowing God is through His Son Jesus Christ, then precisely how do we enter into a relationship with Him? There are three simple steps. I call them the ABC of Christianity. Accept. Believe. Confess.

Take the first: *accept*. This involves accepting the fact that you have fallen short of God's standards and that you can do nothing to save yourself. The Bible tells us that "all have sinned and fall short of the glory of God" (Rom. 3:23). Some people find it difficult to accept the fact that they are sinners. They say, "I have not committed any crimes. I pay my way and don't defraud anyone" or, "I give to charitable work and try to help anyone who needs it . . . so how can I be a sinner?"

Sin is defined by the dictionary as "an act of transgression against divine law." The sin that every one of us must admit to is that even though God made us for a relationship with Himself, we have made no attempt to engage with Him and have kept Him out of our hearts. We have fallen short of His standards and expectations, and admitting and accepting this fact is the very first step on the path to finding God.

The second step is this: *believe*. It involves believing that Jesus Christ is God in human form, that He died on a cross to save you, that He rose again from the dead in order that He might be a living Savior, and that He is the only way to God. The kind of believing I am talking about here is not just an intellectual belief but a heartfelt conviction that this is something that has to be ventured upon.

There is a fascinating story about Blondin, the tightrope walker, who once slung a wire across Niagara Falls and walked across it. When he came down the ladder on the Canadian side of the falls, he saw a little boy in the crowd who seemed mesmerized by the event. He paused as he walked by him and said: "Do you believe I could carry you across the falls on my shoulders?" "Oh yes, sir," answered the little boy. "Then jump up," instructed Blondin. "No

fear," retorted the little boy, pulling back to the safety of his mother's hand. He believed, but there was no committal, no venturing, no trust. To believe in Jesus Christ means you place your life in His hands and trust Him to forgive your sin, give you the gift of eternal life, and introduce you to God.

And the third step? *Confess.* This means telling someone, like a family member or close friend, that you have committed your life to Jesus Christ and that

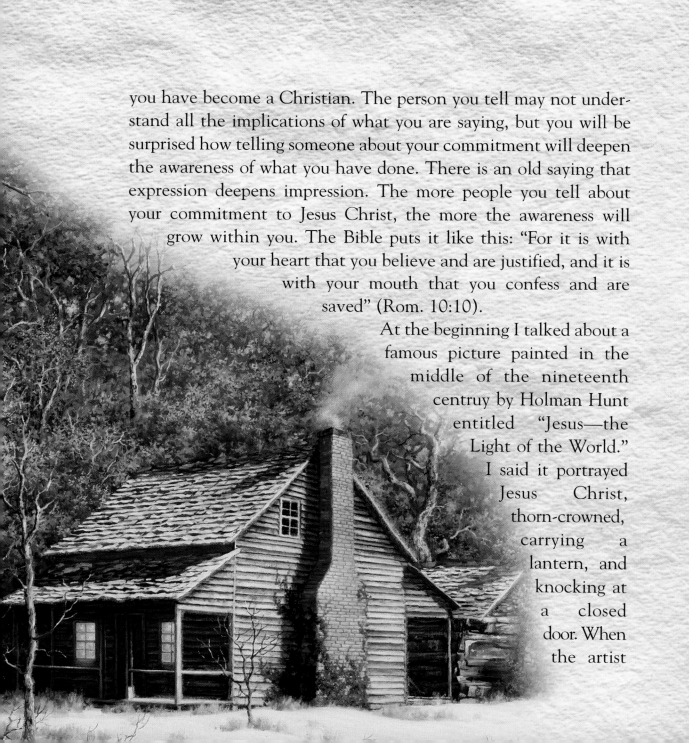

you have become a Christian. The person you tell may not understand all the implications of what you are saying, but you will be surprised how telling someone about your commitment will deepen the awareness of what you have done. There is an old saying that expression deepens impression. The more people you tell about your commitment to Jesus Christ, the more the awareness will grow within you. The Bible puts it like this: "For it is with your heart that you believe and are justified, and it is with your mouth that you confess and are saved" (Rom. 10:10).

At the beginning I talked about a famous picture painted in the middle of the nineteenth centruy by Holman Hunt entitled "Jesus—the Light of the World." I said it portrayed Jesus Christ, thorn-crowned, carrying a lantern, and knocking at a closed door. When the artist showed the completed picture to some friends, someone pointed out what seemed to be an omission. "You have put no handle on the door," he said to Holman Hunt. The artist replied: "We must open to the light; the handle is on the inside."

Jesus Christ cannot come into your life unless you are willing to let Him come in. The handle is on the inside of your soul. If you have never turned your life over to God and would like to do so, then I have framed below a special prayer which, if it helps, you yourself can pray. I can supply the words—you supply the willingness:

> O God my Father, I come to you now through Your Son Jesus Christ. Thank You for speaking to me through the things I have read in this book. I accept the fact I have kept You out of my life for so long, but now, believing that Jesus Christ died for me on the cross, I open the door of my soul to let You in. Forgive my sin, give me the gift of eternal life and, above all, give me the assurance that You have heard my prayer and accepted me. Help me be strong enough to tell others what I have done today. I ask all this in and through the Name of Your Son Jesus Christ.

Without doubt, Jesus Christ never uttered a more marvelous statement than when, in the midst of a world full of spiritual darkness, He stood and said, "I am light of the world."

Sources

1. Eugene Peterson, *Living the Message* (San Francisco: HarperCollins, 1996).

2. E. Stanley Jones, in the Preface to *The Way* (London: Hodder & Stoughton, 1947).

3. Quoted by Alister McGrath in *Bridge Building* (IVP, p. 20).

4. William Watson, in a poem entitled "World Strangeness."

5. W. E. Sangster, in *Westminster Sermons No. 2* (London: Epworth Press, 1961).

Brief Biographies
Selwyn Hughes

Born in Wales to Christian parents who were significantly impacted by the Welsh revivals, Selwyn Hughes trained in theology and counseling in both Britain and the United States. During his eighteen years of pastoring churches around the United Kingdom, he was asked by a few of his congregation to share his method of daily Bible study. From this inconspicuous start grew *Every Day with Jesus*™ and for thirty years Selwyn has authored these daily Bible notes that are read by some 500,000 people around the world. In addition to writing, Selwyn travels extensively in many countries representing a wide range of seminars on different aspects of the Christian life including counseling, marriage, relationships, and personal development.

Larry Dyke

Success came hard for Larry Dyke. After attending Baylor University on an athletic scholarship and teaching junior high school for a few years, he found himself frustrated with the course of his life. The loss of a child in the late sixties dealt a sorrowful blow to him and his family.

A few years later, Dyke left teaching and began making the rounds of galleries with his paintings. The second gallery he visited took his work on consignment, but Dyke had little hope for success.

"This was one of the lowest points of my life," he recalls. "I felt God had forsaken me. Just when I was feeling that, however, the phone rang. It was the gallery owner. He had just sold several paintings and said he wanted more. I knew this was what the Lord wanted me to do." Today Dyke's paintings hang in the White House, the Vatican, and the homes of distinguished personalities including Billy and Ruth Graham.

Dyke's genius is that he can construct intricate settings even the untutored art lover appreciates. His collectors are attracted by a grassroots admiration for traditional realistic painting.

Larry Dyke is a native Texan who has traveled, often with his wife and daughter, to some of the world's most beautiful places. Underlying his painting is his deep Christian faith. "When I became a full-time artist, I was impressed to put a scriptural notation on each of my paintings," Dyke states. "It's an expression of what I think the true answer to life is."

Christian faith has much to do with the quality of Larry Dyke's work. His dramatic landscapes are suffused with a calm spirituality and signed with a trademark Bible verse. "I can't separate my faith from my painting," he says. "When I became a full-time artist, I began to put a scriptural notation on each of my paintings. It's an expression of what I think the true answer to life is."